CONTENTS

Something strange happened to British Pop Music in 1995. For the first time in God-knows-how-long there was a song at number 1 in the singles chart that was played by a REAL group! The song was "Some Might Say" and the group was, of course, Oasis. You see, prior to that single, the charts had become a bit of a joke. I suppose it's true to say that they still are, but at least this song (and of course the band itself) gave us all a ray of hope.

Once upon a time, the singles chart was full of real bands reflecting the sort of music that real people were listening to and buying. I often wonder what it must have been like to listen to a chart show and hear a Top Ten featuring The Beatles, The Rolling Stones, The Kinks, The Who and maybe the odd record by Diana Ross or someone like that. Those days are long gone and ever since I can remember, the charts have been nothing more than a vehicle for promoting artists and influencing people's tastes (not REFLECTING people's tastes).

Real bands have been very scarce in the Pop world in recent years. The charts have been pretty much dominated by M.C. this or D.J. that and, more often than not, "Featuring-who-gives-a-shit?" The situation has changed dramatically since THAT song was sitting on top of our singles chart and in my opinion, long may it continue. I'm into real bands; they don't have to be the greatest bands of all time, just real guys (or girls!) playing real instruments and writing real songs. It's not much to ask for but in the sampled, synthesised, dance-dominated 90's, real bands very nearly became an endangered species.

Enter Oasis, the new saviours of Rock and Roll! Well, I don't know about that, but I do know that ever since these five guys from Manchester came on the scene, it's been cool to be into real bands and watch real guys playing guitars and drums and stuff like that. And I am into that! Oasis have pretty much changed the general public's perception of what Pop Music is. Yeah, they play guitars but they're not Heavy Metal. Yeah, they've got attitude (in abundance!) but they're not Punk or Rap. Yeah, they've got loads of catchy songs but they're not a Teen Boy Band. They're just a bunch of real guys playing real music and it seems that real people want to hear them.

Perhaps even more important than that is the fact that not only do people want hear them, but they want to hear ABOUT them. In fact, it seems that the public love hearing about the various antics and exploits of people in or connected to Oasis. The Gallagher brothers are almost permanent fixtures in today's newspapers, whether it be their latest bust-up, or their latest bust, or their latest outrageous comments or their latest outrageous comments about the press! The

Gallaghers ARE news and have been for quite a while, however now it seems that the likes of Patsy Kensit and even "Bonehead" are in demand by the news mongers of our time. These days, merely knowing a Gallagher seems to make you newsworthy.

From a personal point of view, I like Oasis. I don't claim to be their greatest fan but nevertheless, over the last few years I've heard the stories, read the newspapers and most importantly of all, listened to the music. It's impossible to live in the U.K. and not know anything about them. I also think it's impossible to not be at least a little enchanted by their behaviour and rapidly-developing "legend". Oasis are pretty much the band everyone has dreamed of being in; loud, arrogant, controversial, fashionable, unfashionable, sex, drugs and Rock and Roll. Oh, and by the way, they've sold quite a few records too! And all in the space of a few years. It seems quite incredible when you think about it. I don't think there has ever been a group which has risen to the top as rapidly as Oasis. It's almost impossible to write a history of Oasis because they haven't been around long enough! Almost impossible, but not actually impossible as you're about to find out.

And so the Oasis saga goes on and on. It is a story that I'm sure has a very long way to go yet. All we can do is sit back and watch nature take it's course. They might self-destruct at any moment and there's nothing anyone can do about it. In fact, bearing in mind the Gallagher brothers' history of intense rivalry bordering on hatred, it's quite an achievement that they've lasted as long as they have. Whether Oasis as a band have the stability to remain in existence for any long period of time, we just don't know. But I'm sure we'll have a great time finding out! Perhaps that's the greatest aspect of Oasis, their almost cartoon-like lifestyle. They are the archetypal rock band; we love to hate them but we also just love them too.

So while reading this book remember, by the time you've finished it Oasis may be no more! Or they just may be even bigger than they were when you started reading! That's the sort of band they are. They never cease to amaze us, the watching public and I'm sure they amaze themselves sometimes too. Definitely, err, maybe, err....

DAVID RICHTER
Rock Music Journalist

Noel Gallagher was born on May 29th, 1967 to parents Peggy and Tommy. Liam Gallagher was born on September 21st, 1972. Both the Gallagher brothers went to St. Bernard's Primary School and then to The Barlow Roman Catholic High School where their mother worked as a dinner lady. They lived in the Burnage area of Manchester and most of their school days were dominated by Manchester City Football Club whom they both loved (and still do) with a passion. Their love of football was to play a major part in the formation of Oasis but let's not jump the gun just yet!

Neither brother had a particularly outstanding academic career; it appears that from an early age they both knew that their destiny lay elsewhere. According to the man himself, Noel Gallagher first strummed a guitar at the age of eight years old. The first song he is reputed to have learned was "The House Of The Rising Sun" by The Animals. Liam, as you have probably worked out, was all of three years old at this time!

The first song that Noel ever wrote was called "Badges". It was about the people who wore them. Noel was thirteen years old at the time and he's never looked back since. In 1983, parents Peggy and Tommy divorced which resulted in Tommy leaving the family home. During this time, both Noel and Liam were regulars in the gangs of kids who played football on the local Burnage pitches (which are also said to be ripe with "magic mushrooms" although it is unconfirmed that this was an incentive for the Gallaghers to play there).

Many kids from the local music scene also played football on the Burnage pitches including Paul Bardsley (ex-Molly Half Head) who formed an early "band" with Noel called "Fantasy Chicken And The Amateurs". It was at one of these infamous kickabouts that Noel and Liam met up with Tony McCarroll, Paul "Guigsy" McGuigan and Paul "Bonehead" Arthurs. These three went on to form The Rain, a Manchester-based band including Chris Hutton on lead vocals. They didn't know it at the time but these five football-mad kids were to be seeing a lot more of each other in the not too distant future.

In December 1988, Noel auditioned for the role of lead singer with Manchester's legendary Inspiral Carpets. Unfortunately he wasn't quite what they were looking for at the time but they were impressed with him and offered him another job, as their chief roadie! He took this job and subsequently quit his full-time job as a Gas Board watchman at the Manchester City Centre Depot. Noel's new job took him on tour with "the Inspirals" and not only was he on good money, but he learned a great deal. He was included in a lot of business with the Inspirals and struck up a friendship with their engineer, Mark Coyle. He was also writing his own songs seriously by this time and his time with the Inspirals is widely regarded as Noel's first "break" in the music business (even though many people regard being a roadie as a waste of time!).

It was on Noel's return from a long tour of the U.S. with the Inspiral Carpets when he learned that in his absence, Liam had been a busy boy himself! As well as taking over Noel's vacant job at the Gas Board, Liam had also got himself involved

with The Rain, having promised the other members that he'd involve Noel in the band if they got rid of singer Chris Hutton and took himself as lead singer. This they agreed to even though Liam had not informed his brother of recent events. As a result of all this, The Rain (who had by now changed their name to Oasis) had to play their first gig without Noel. This took place at The Boardwalk, Manchester, on August 18th, 1991. Certain members of the Inspiral Carpets were in the audience along with Paul Gallagher (the third Gallagher brother) and a highly critical Noel.

After seeing the band, Noel told them exactly what he thought. He said that although they had no decent songs, they did have some potential and he was willing to consider joining them if they let him write all the songs and work out the musical aspect of the band. He also told them that if they had any hopes of going fully-professional, they would have to work much harder. He told them that he would only join the band if they got serious and "went for it". This would mean working six days a week to get things right, rehearsing, gigging and recording. Noel saw working with a band as a full-time job, not a hobby to occupy your weekends or odd nights mid-week. Noel was right and it didn't take long for the rest of the band to agree; Noel was now a proper part of Oasis.

The naming of Oasis is a story in itself. Both Paul and Noel Gallagher have their own versions. According to Paul Gallagher, the name Oasis came from a venue in Swindon, The Swindon Oasis. According to Noel Gallagher, the name came from a local shop in Manchester where he and his friends bought trainers and T-shirts. Whichever story is correct, the band didn't actually adopt the name until Liam took over as lead singer.

Oasis, with Noel in charge, began rehearsing frequently at rehearsal rooms underneath The Boardwalk venue. Along with various other local bands such as Dub Sex, The New Fast Automatic Daffodils and Detox, Oasis worked hard getting their music together and are rumoured to have been involved in a great rivalry which even saw some groups bricking up the doorways to each other's rehearsal space! Legend has it that Oasis were actually quite civilised in these matters with the major feud taking place between Detox and The New Fast Automatic Daffodils. One thing was for sure, Oasis were getting better and the hard work was starting to pay off. It was now time for Noel to lead his troops into the recording studio to make a demo.

The first Oasis demo was recorded at the Abraham Moss studios just before Christmas 1991. Noel later denied that he actually played on it, claiming he was responsible just for the compositions and that he was "involved" in the production. Paul Gallagher claims that Noel DID play on it but was embarrassed because it didn't come out as well as he would have liked. The demo was played on local radio stations although no one was really that impressed with it and it did get reviewed in the local Manchester magazine City Life. Despite this, the tape did get Liam noticed by a local D.J. who wanted him to join the band that he managed, That Uncertain Feeling. That never happened and Oasis carried on working into the New Year as before. In January 1992, Oasis played their first gig with Noel Gallagher at The Boardwalk. The first song they played was an instrumental version of "Columbia" (a song which later appeared on their first album). With Noel's experience and songwriting, they couldn't possibly fail....could they?

OASIS OASIS OA
SIS OASIS OAS
OASIS OASIS OA
OASIS OASIS OA
SIS OASIS OAS
OASIS OASIS OA

The Oasis story is one of hard work and being in the right place at the right time. However things could have turned out very different if, in the summer of 1992, they had agreed to appear on a Factory Records compilation album. Manchester label Factory Records were the first record company to really show any interest in the band, the problem was that at the time Factory was getting dangerously close to bankruptcy. Clint Boon of the Inspirals was responsible for introducing Oasis to Factory Records and after seeing them live at (once again!) The Boardwalk, Factory's Phil Saxe wanted to get them on a compilation "sampler". The deal fell through and many people think it was probably for the best as Oasis were still in their early development and Factory Records had their own problems to contend with. Still, it must have been nice to know that even though they didn't have a record deal yet, someone was interested in their music.

By this time, not only were Oasis starting to attract record company interest but they were also starting to attract the interest of the music press. In June 1992, music journalist Penny Anderson of The Manchester Evening News interviewed the band. This was their second ever interview and their first interview with a major publication. In the interview Noel explained that they wanted to add a keyboard player to the group line-up but they didn't because there's never been a keyboard player who looks cool on stage - apart from Elton John! The interview went under the title "Just when the music scene was drying up.... The refreshing sounds of Oasis".

In July 1992, Oasis recorded their first live radio session. It was for a Radio 5 show being put together by D.J. Mark Radcliffe called "Hit The North". Rumour has it that the B.B.C. have since lost the tapes of these sessions which is a shame as I've heard that they contain the original version of "Cigarettes And Alcohol", amongst others.

Although Oasis were working hard (Noel had warned them they'd have to) and had begun to get some sort of recognition for their efforts, it was in many ways the same old story; they had no money! They had done a few recordings, played a few gigs and rehearsed a lot but were not making enough money to call themselves "professional" musicians. It's at this time in most other band's careers that they usually split up - they just can't afford to carry on. Noel was lucky. Towards the end of 1992 he was offered another roadie job with the Inspirals and he just couldn't turn it down. The chance to earn some decent money again was too tempting and Noel toured Europe with the Inspirals for two months. After this tour the Inspirals sacked their entire road crew (including Noel) because they were fed up with their roadie's drug-taking exploits. They were sad to see Noel go because he was a good friend of the band but after receiving a "golden handshake", Noel's Inspiral Carpets days were over. Noel later admitted that he probably deserved the sack (his infamous "drug-smuggling" stories have become part of the Inspirals legend!) and as it turned out, leaving the Inspirals once and for all was probably the best thing that happened to him at this stage in his career. For Noel Gallagher it was now Oasis or bust!

In December 1992, Oasis returned to the studio to record another demo. Oasis and Noel in particular had become very friendly with Liverpool-based band Real People, who had set up their own recording studio in Liverpool. It was only an eight-track set up and the band (especially Liam) were still quite raw, but with the help of Real People's Tony Griffiths and his brother Chris, as well as three months labouring on the demo, they eventually came away with their most significant piece of work thus far - Live Demonstration. Most of the songs on this recording eventually appeared either on Oasis singles as B-sides, or on the album "Definitely Maybe". Included on this demo were the songs "Cloudburst", "Rock'n'Roll Star", "Married With Children" and "Fade Away".

By this time Oasis had done very little outside of Manchester and Liverpool, but in May 1993 their next big break occurred, in Glasgow of all places! On May 18th, Oasis played a gig at King Tut's Wah Wah Hut in Glasgow, Scotland. Many people regard this as the gig that "made" Oasis. The headlining band that night was actually 18 Wheeler and Oasis weren't even on the bill! Sister Lovers, a band who shared Oasis's rehearsal space at The Boardwalk were the support act for this gig and when they found out that the venue needed another support band, they took Oasis along with them on the night, unannounced! Oasis turned up only to be told that the venue management had found a third band and they wouldn't let Oasis play. This third band was Boyfriend who were friends with Sister Lovers. Sister Lovers told the promoter that they wouldn't play if Oasis didn't play first and Boyfriend told the promoter that they wouldn't play unless Sister Lovers played first. A frantic promoter tried to eject Oasis from the premises but Noel pointed out that if his band didn't play, then both Sister Lovers and Boyfriend together with fifteen or so Oasis supporters would be extremely upset and "it's going to kick-off!" What could the poor guy do? Oasis were eventually permitted a twenty minute slot at the foot of the bill and according to Noel, it was the worst gig they had ever done! Still, it was the repercussions which have made this event one of the most important in the history of Oasis.

Oasis only got to play four songs that night. One of them was a cover of The Beatles classic "I Am The Walrus". There were about seven people in the audience. However, one of those people happened to be Creation Records boss Alan McGee. He had actually turned up to see 18 Wheeler but was very impressed with Oasis. He liked what he saw, especially Liam Gallagher who he thought looked really cool, like a "northern Paul Weller". He offered the band a deal almost immediately although they weren't initially all that interested. Noel gave him a copy of Live Demonstration after the gig. Very soon after this, Noel, Liam and Bonehead were on a train heading to London to visit Creation Records. When our intrepid trio from Manchester finally arrived at Creation's offices they immediately saw a big problem. The company M.D. Tim Abbott was wearing a Manchester United shirt and both Noel and Liam, being fanatical Manchester City supporters, couldn't possibly do business with either him or his colleagues until he removed the offending item of clothing.

By June it was becoming clear that Oasis would sign to Creation, the problem was that at this time they still had no management. Through a chance meeting between Noel and a friend, the Live Demonstration demo ended up being heard by Johnny Marr, Noel's hero and guitarist with The Smiths. Johnny contacted Noel and after discussing their shared love of vintage guitars, he agreed to talk to his manager about what they might do for Oasis. Johnny Marr and his manager, Marcus Russell, saw Oasis play live at the Hop And Grape in Manchester, supporting Dodgy in June 1993. No contract has ever bound Oasis to Russell's management company Ignition Management, however Marcus Russell has handled Oasis ever since that gig. News was starting to spread of this new band that both Creation Records and Ignition Management were involved with and it wasn't long before other companies were trying to muscle their way in....

On September 14th, 1993, Oasis played a Creation showcase gig at the Canal Cafe Bar in Manchester. Other bands on the bill that night included 18 Wheeler and Medalark 11. On October 22nd, Oasis signed a six album deal with Creation Records in the U.K., they also signed a world-wide distribution deal with Sony. By November of the same year, Oasis were on tour. They were supporting some of the biggest names in the Indie world including Saint Etienne, The Verve, Liz Phair and The Milltown Brothers. On December 16th, Oasis supported Real People at The Krazy House in Liverpool.

The connection between Oasis and Real People was further solidified when following the Krazy House gig, Creation booked Oasis into The Pink Museum studio and they took Real People along with them to produce these sessions. It was during these three days of recordings that Real People's Tony Griffiths told Noel to write a decent song instead of just playing "a pile of shite". Noel responded by making a song out of a "Neil Young-type jam". The song was "Supersonic". It was also during this time that Creation began marketing Oasis with a big promotional push. The song "Columbia", now complete with lyrics, was released on it's own as a white label, strictly for radio air play. Creation's plugging team achieved the impossible: getting B.B.C. Radio 1 to play this song even though it wasn't commercially available, it hadn't been released as a single. Never before had

Radio 1 play-listed a song that wasn't on sale in record shops, until now. Creation deserved great credit for this and immediately recognised the potential of what they had done.

Maintaining this new-found momentum, Creation sent Oasis to Mono Valley Studios in Monmouth, South Wales. They arrived on January 7th, 1994. They didn't actually achieve a great deal here although they did bump into The Stone Roses in Monmouth! After eighteen days of very little action, Oasis moved to London's Olympic Studios. That was even worse! After a mere four days they decided to leave and got rid of producer Dave Bachelor. Then they moved to the Sawmills Studios in Cornwall with producer Mark Coyle (from Noel's Inspiral Carpets days). During a ten day period in February they recorded most of the songs that eventually ended up on the album "Definitely Maybe".

The first truly controversial incident which Oasis became involved with took place on February 18th, 1994. They were travelling on a ferry to Amsterdam, to play a gig supporting The Verve. When they arrived in The Netherlands only Noel was allowed to leave the port. The others were all being detained in a dockyard cell. According to reliable sources, while Noel was asleep his Oasis colleagues were all involved in a drinking session that got completely out of control and ended up in a fight between themselves (Manchester City supporters) and a bunch of Chelsea fans. The gig had to be cancelled and the first of many disagreements between Noel and Liam spilled over into an N.M.E. interview. A disgruntled Noel accused his brother of being "like some scouse schleppers with handcuffs". This was the first of many such incidents and the first public row between the two brothers, the best was yet to come!

At the end of March, Oasis made their television debut on the Channel 4 music show The Word. The impact was incredible with Oasis gigs selling out regularly, purely on the strength of their one and only television appearance. On April 11th, the first eagerly-awaited single was released. "Supersonic" was the track and the combination of a good song, a much talked-about T.V. appearance, more live work, a good video and the support of the N.M.E. ensured that it made the Top 40, peaking at number 31. Oasis were on their way at last.

The summer of 1994 saw some significant events take place in the Oasis story. The second single, "Shakermaker" was released on June 20th. The immediate reaction from anyone hearing this song for the first time is that it's a direct rip-off of the old song "I'd Like To Teach The World To Sing" which was adopted for a famous T.V. advert in the 70's. Noel has never denied this and even though many people accuse Oasis of being little more than Beatles-wannabes, at least this song proves that they have other "influences" too! Shakermaker took Oasis to just outside the Top 10, peaking at number 11 in the singles chart.

The band's profile was dramatically raised in this month following two more T.V. appearances. The first was an obligatory showing on B.B.C. Television's Top Of The Pops. This boosted sales for the current single and also helped to promote their other main event of June 1994. On June 26th, Oasis played at the Glastonbury Festival and were part of Channel 4's "4 Goes To Glastonbury". Oasis played on the N.M.E. stage and their set was between Credit To The Nation and Echobelly.

Noel almost missed the start of the show but legend has it that Liam "sorted him out" and as a result, Oasis went down a storm.

A month after Glastonbury, Oasis made a brief journey to the U.S.A. For Noel, the outstanding highlight of this trip was a visit to Strawberry Fields, the John Lennon memorial park in New York. Then on August 8th, the next Oasis single was released. "Live Forever" was the band's first Top 10 hit (just!), peaking at number 10. They had planned with Creation to release one single every other month and to promote each song so that it reached a slightly higher chart position than the last one. At this point in time their plan was working.

By now the hype surrounding Oasis in the music press was reaching fever pitch. The encouraging chart success of their first three singles together with their live reputation (helped considerably by the Glastonbury show) and of course the ever-growing fascination of the press with their behaviour and comments (which by now were getting more and more outrageous!) all helped to generate a buzz which had not been felt since The Sex Pistols. Oasis were on the front pages of music papers and expectations were running very high as their debut album was due to be released.

"Definitely Maybe" was released on August 29th, 1994. It cost around £75,000 to make and saw the band using a massive seven different studios to record and produce it. It quickly became the fastest selling debut album of all time, shifting some 150,000 copies in the first couple of days following it's release. Definitely Maybe entered the U.K. album chart at number 1. The band played acoustic versions of "Supersonic", "Live Forever", "Shakermaker", "Slide Away", "Whatever" and "Sad Song" in London's Virgin Megastore at Marble Arch on the day of it's release. Over a thousand Oasis fans were in attendance.

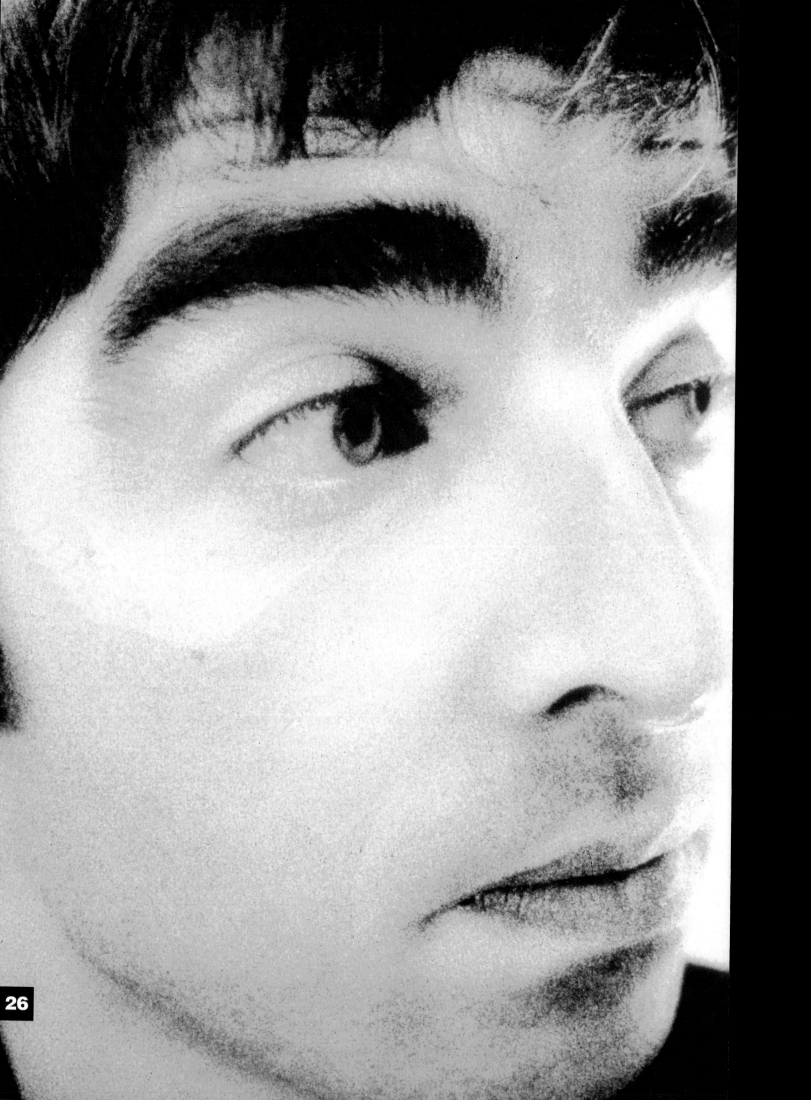

1994 had been a big year for Oasis. Not only had they recorded their first album and experienced their first taste of chart success, they had also made their first television appearances and played their first festival and the year wasn't even over yet! Following hot on the release and success of the album Definitely Maybe, Oasis travelled to Japan to play their first live dates in that part of the world. When they arrived, in September 1994, even they couldn't have anticipated the reception that was waiting for them. To say that the Japanese fans were "mad for it" would be an enormous understatement.

Oasis had never released a record in Japan and yet all the dates sold out within hours of being announced. When they arrived at the airport they were mobbed by hoards of screaming girls wearing Manchester City Football Club shirts! Not even Noel or Liam could possibly have expected to see that. They were also given presents by the fans including footballs and Beatles bootlegs. Oasis had truly gone international in every sense of the word. It was only a short tour but it couldn't have gone better and at the last night in Nagoya, Oasis played their first ever encore (well better late than never!).

Oasis returned to sunny Manchester for three days before embarking on

their next mission for world domination: The U.S.A. (if they could make it there they'd make it, well, just about anywhere....) Unfortunately this attempt at world domination didn't go as well as the Japanese tour. The band were ejected from Johnny Depp's infamous Viper Room, then Bonehead was cautioned for disturbing the peace, Liam hit Noel on stage with a tambourine, Liam and Bonehead were confronted by a gun-toting gentleman and then Noel flew home on his own after another argument with the rest of the band. All in all, a pretty rough time was had by everyone.

Oasis returned home to much better news. Their latest single "Cigarettes And Alcohol", which was released on October 10th, was the biggest Oasis hit to date peaking at a rather lofty number 7 in the U.K. singles chart. The biggest problem the band had at home was having to constantly answer the boring old question, "So do you really think you're going to be the next Beatles?" Even in the U.S., questions were being asked about the direction and influences of Noel's song-writing and in one infamous interview with an American radio station, Liam told the public in no uncertain terms that Oasis weren't Mods!

The year ended in the best possible way for the band. On December 12th, the fifth Oasis single was released. "Whatever", with it's orchestral parts was tipped to be a Christmas number 1. That didn't quite happen but it did prove to be the next big Oasis hit, peaking at number 3. Interestingly enough this song was the centre of a new controversy as it was claimed that it was a Bowie-esque rip-off of Mott The Hoople's "All The Young Dudes". Lawyers were consulted and with one minor change of lyrics (removing the line "all the young blues"), the song was released and became a hit. This song was also the first recording Oasis had made since the Definitely Maybe sessions. It proved to be an incredible end to an incredible year for the band but in time-honoured tradition, the best was yet to come....

Oasis started 1995 in the same way they had finished the previous year. Following the success of Whatever, Noel spent much of January writing an entire batch of new songs on his acoustic guitar. The next few months were spent on another U.S. tour in a desperate attempt to make up for their disappointment of the previous year. There were various breaks during this tour which allowed the band to return to the U.K. to do some recording and to collect some much-deserved awards. On February 22nd, the band arrived at the Loco studio in Wales to record their next single, "Some Might Say". According to reliable sources, on the way to the studio Noel's train experienced a twenty minute delay and in this time he wrote one of the songs on the "B-side". The song in question was "Acquiesce". On Tuesday February 28th, Oasis attended the British music industry award ceremony, The Brits. Although they won the "best new band" award, the show was actually dominated by their arch-enemies Blur who collected four awards (well there's no accounting for taste is there?). The U.S. tour finished on March 25th and was much more successful than before. The band could return home extremely happy, safe in the knowledge that America was finally getting the message.

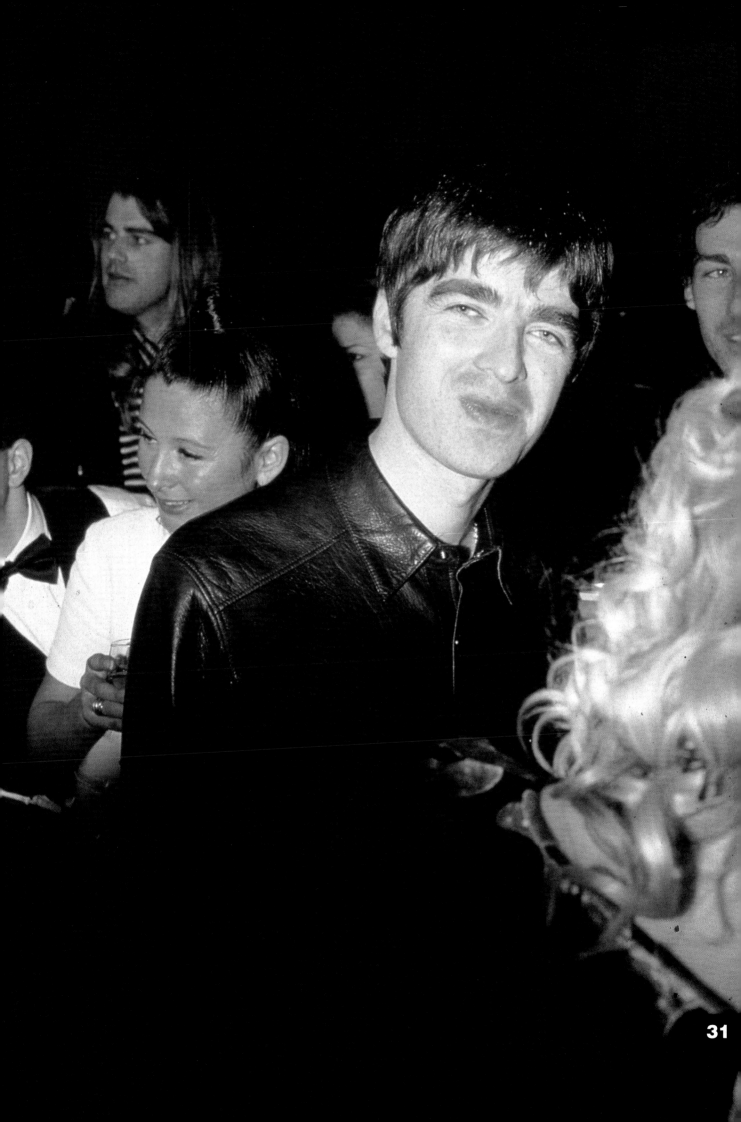

The new single, "Some Might Say", was released on April 24th, 1995. This proved to be their greatest achievement to date as it was the band's first number 1 hit. It cemented their position as THE band in the U.K. and further fuelled the Oasis mania which was sweeping the country. Three days after it's release and following a fight in a hotel with Liam, drummer Tony McCarroll was no longer a part of Oasis. Apparently this was a personnel problem that had been "brewing" for some time and Tony's last appearance with Oasis was on Top Of The Pops.

Oasis needed a replacement drummer and fast! Tony McCarroll's successor was a 22 year-old Londoner, Alan White. Alan's brother Steve had established quite a reputation for himself playing with Paul Weller, now it was Alan's turn. Alan White's debut appearance with Oasis was on Thursday May 4th, once more on Top Of The Pops.

Oasis returned to the recording studio with their new band member to make their second album on May 8th. Some Might Say was still at number 1 and the band started this project on an understandable high. These sessions took place at Rockfield Studios, Wales. The entire album from songwriting to production was very much Noel's "baby" and there were numerous fights within the band during this time (especially between Noel and Liam). At one stage Noel "quit", claiming that the rest of the band were unprofessional and that he couldn't carry on. He went to stay with footballer Graham Le Saux in Jersey for a week, before return-

ing to face the music (quite literally!). The album was co-produced with Owen Morris who seemed permanently mystified by Noel's love/hate relationship with his brother. No matter how much arguing and fighting took place between Noel and Liam (or anyone else for that matter), they always seemed to make up eventually and return to work. Noel and Owen are alleged to have worked some fifteen or more hours a day in order to get the recording right, only involving other band members when it was really necessary. This was obviously a formula which they used before and being familiar with it, it was now starting to pay off. The new album took just over one month to complete.

On June 23rd, Oasis returned to Glastonbury to headline at the festival. This time it was quite disappointing however. Noel had a bad cold and Liam got into a fight with just about everyone else! The only high point came when the band were joined by Robbie Williams on stage (this appearance marked the end of Robbie's connection with Take That). After the show there were more confrontations involving Liam and a "a group of rugby players". As previously stated, this was not a day that Oasis cherish fond memories of. Oasis then headed off to Europe for a tour which took in over six countries.

The seventh Oasis single was released on August 14th, 1995. Amidst a blaze of publicity, Oasis attempted to reproduce the success of their last single which topped the chart. The song being offered was "Roll With It". Everything was set for the biggest Oasis hit single to date; good song, slick video, loads of promotion, sorted. Well, not quite. What followed in the next few weeks was a battle, the likes of which had not been seen for some 30 years, ever since the days of the rivalry between The Beatles and The Rolling Stones! This time it was even fiercer as Oasis were forced into all-out war with Blur.

Upon learning the release date for Roll With It, Blur's label brought forward the release date of their next single, "Country House". Both songs were released on the same day and the nation held it's breath as the new kings of the south, Blur, took on the might of the north, Oasis. Both sides launched vicious attacks on each other and the music press lapped it all up with glee. The rivalry soon became front page news as the national press became obsessed with this new "Battle of the Bands". It wasn't long before the most talked-about subject of the time was, "Do you prefer Roll With It or Country House?" The debate was further fuelled by Liam's much-publicised attempt to lure away Damon Albarn's girlfriend, Justine Frischman (of Elastica fame). Blur's singer was alleged to have had a run-in with Noel at a party and it all got totally out of control. Creation Records, Food (Blur's label), the music press, the national press and even the bookies (!) were loving every minute of this and it was with great anticipation that the chart positions were announced. Despite making most of the early running (especially in the north), Roll With It entered the singles chart at number 2. Not bad eh? Well the problem was that in the same week, Country House entered the singles chart at number 1! Blur had won.

Noel was not impressed and very soon afterwards, the sparks really did fly. Firstly Noel accused Creation Records of gross incompetence, claiming that they had mixed up the bar codes on the single and thus lost Oasis valuable ground in

their fight with Blur. He said that despite all of his hard work and the work that the rest of the band had put in, Creation simply "weren't up to it". Then in an interview with The Observer newspaper, Noel said of Damon Albarn and Alex James (Blur's singer and bass player respectively) that he wished the pair of them would catch AIDS and die! After calming down and realising what he'd said, he later apologised to everyone concerned. The point that everyone seemed to miss at the time (including both Blur and Oasis) was that with the publicity generated by these events and the media frenzy that ensued, the real winners of this "contest" were Blur AND Oasis. Interestingly enough, it should be pointed out that Roll With It was the biggest selling Oasis single to date even though it didn't reach number 1. Still, you can't win 'em all....

Oasis then played a short seven-date tour of Japan at the end of August. The next month was eventful in a strange sort of way as Bonehead got married, a Bournemouth show was cancelled (because Blur booked a gig in the town on the same day!) and grieving Take That fans accused Oasis of causing the rift between Robbie Williams and the rest of the group! Worse was to come as Paul "Guigsy" McGuigan announced he would not be going on the upcoming British tour because he was not in a fit state to go on the road (he was exhausted). Dates had to be rescheduled and Noel announced that the band could be finished if they didn't find a suitable replacement.

Guigsy was ordered to rest by his doctor and Scott McLeod of fellow Manchester band The Ya Yas was eventually offered the job for a six-month period. Oasis had dates lined up in the U.K., Europe and The U.S.A. so it was vital that this matter was resolved as soon as possible. On October 2nd, 1995, the next Oasis album was released. "(What's The Story) Morning Glory?", the eagerly-awaited follow up to Definitely Maybe, entered the U.K. album chart at number 1. It sold over 350,000 units in it's first week and became the fastest selling album since Michael Jackson's "BAD". Noel was especially pleased with it and was soon receiving heaped praise for his songwriting. Yeah, there were still some questions surrounding "borrowed" ideas (including The Small Faces, The Kinks and you've guessed it, The Beatles!), but Noel was being hailed as the new songwriting genius of his generation. Okay, let's not go overboard, Morning Glory is a good album but it's not that good, or is it? Well the inevitable journalistic gushings amplified the hype to epic proportions and pretty soon, you couldn't move for Oasis interviews, T.V. appearances, posters etc....

Interesting facts about the new album: "Step Out" was pulled from the album when Stevie Wonder demanded 6% royalties from the entire album for the tracks' similarity to his own song "Uptight". "Bonehead's Bank Holiday" was an extra track, only available on the vinyl version and features Bonehead on lead vocals. "Wonderwall" is the title of a George Harrison album and "Don't Look Back In Anger" has an introduction "borrowed" from John Lennon's "Imagine".

The extraordinary success of the Morning Glory album finally laid the Oasis/Blur argument to rest. Blur had won the initial singles battle, but surely now it could not be denied that Oasis had won the album war. (What's The Story) Morning Glory far outstripped Blur's "The Great Escape" as a strong contender for Album Of The Decade. Oasis mania was back and bigger than before.

On October 7th, Oasis returned to the U.S.A. It was Scott McLeod's first major assignment with the band and it also proved to be his last! On October 17th, following a concert in Buffalo, New York, Scott Mcleod quit the tour and returned to the U.K. Once again, after all their recent successes, Oasis were in complete disarray. In the wake of this disaster they did manage to complete one gig as a four-piece with Bonehead taking over as replacement bass player. It couldn't work for long however and the group returned to Britain with two sold out dates at Earl's Court, London, to contend with and still no solution to the bass player problem. Noel decided that there was only one thing for it, they had to bring back Guigsy. It took some convincing to coax the still-unwell Paul McGuigan back into action but Noel did the business and on November 4th and 5th, Oasis played at the Earl's Court Exhibition Centre and made history as these shows were the largest indoor music events ever staged in Europe.

Just prior to these shows, on October 30th 1995, the next single to be taken from (What's The Story) Morning Glory, "Wonderwall", was released. Peaking at number 2 in the singles chart, it was aided by the subsequent "cover version" recorded by the Mike Flowers Pops which kept the song in the charts for much longer than it would normally have been. The success of Wonderwall delayed the release date of the next Oasis single and the success of the Wonderwall cover version delighted both the fans and the band themselves who were flattered by it. Wonderwall was the song that finally established Oasis as the band of their generation. With it's obvious Beatle-esque influences and it's anthemic appeal, it once and for all established the songwriting of Noel Gallagher as being amongst the very best there is on offer in today's music scene.

In December, Oasis returned once more to the U.S. to play some shows that were rescheduled as a result of Scott McLeod's quick exit. A still-recovering Guigsy performed heroics on bass guitar and the band were further lifted with the news that Wonderwall had just entered the Billboard chart at number 21 and that the Morning Glory album had sold well over 1 million copies in the U.S. alone. The last U.S. date was played on December 18th and then they returned to the U.K. where Creation Records threw a massive party for them. There was much celebration and present-giving as Creation reflected on their best year so far. Virtually all of Creation's success was due to the monumental efforts of one band in particular, Oasis....

"Someone showed me The House Of The Rising Sun and I never looked back."

NOEL GALLAGHER

"I learnt that you'll get ripped off unless you're very careful. And I learnt that all record company people are twats, bar none."

NOEL GALLAGHER

"I wasn't put on this earth to dig holes."

LIAM GALLAGHER

"Liam was always a cocky little so and so, but I always knew he would make the band happen."

PAUL GALLAGHER

"You pick up your guitar, rip a few people's tunes off, swap them round a bit, get your brother in the band, punch his head in every now and again, and it sells."

NOEL GALLAGHER

"Keyboard players don't look cool onstage, they just keep their heads down. There has never been a cool keyboard player, apart from Elton John."

NOEL GALLAGHER

"Have you heard of Oasis? Well I've just signed them and they're going to be the next Beatles."

ALAN McGEE

"Rock n' Roll is about being yourself. I went on that boat, I had a drink. I had too much beer and I got in a fight, and that was it."

LIAM GALLAGHER

"Me and Bonehead would just walk into a hotel room and empty it out the window."

NOEL GALLAGHER

"It's gone mad! We've had, like, proper stage invasions the last two...f***ing wild!"

LIAM GALLAGHER

"I've done the groupie bit...but I'm not in the band to sleep around. I am in it for two big reasons. I love music and I want to be very rich."

NOEL GALLAGHER

"I'm into the girls fancying me and stuff, mad for it. Get a bit worried if boys started fancying me, definitely. I've got nothing against gays, they do what they do, I do what I do...as long as they don't pinch me on the bum or whatever."

LIAM GALLAGHER

"I suppose I should slow down but I usually go mad for forty days and then I'm sensible for the next forty days. The chest pains and stuff don't bother me. Medical science has come a long way. It's amazing what you can put yourself through and get away with. If my lifestyle ever affected my work I'd clean up, but it doesn't. We don't go on stage when we're out of it, we play totally straight."

NOEL GALLAGHER

"What people have got to understand is that we're lads, we have burgled houses and nicked car stereos, and we like girls and we swear."

NOEL GALLAGHER

"It's weird being in a band with your brother. You go on the road, you live in the same van, then you go to your mam's for Sunday lunch and he's there. It's HELL!"

NOEL GALLAGHER

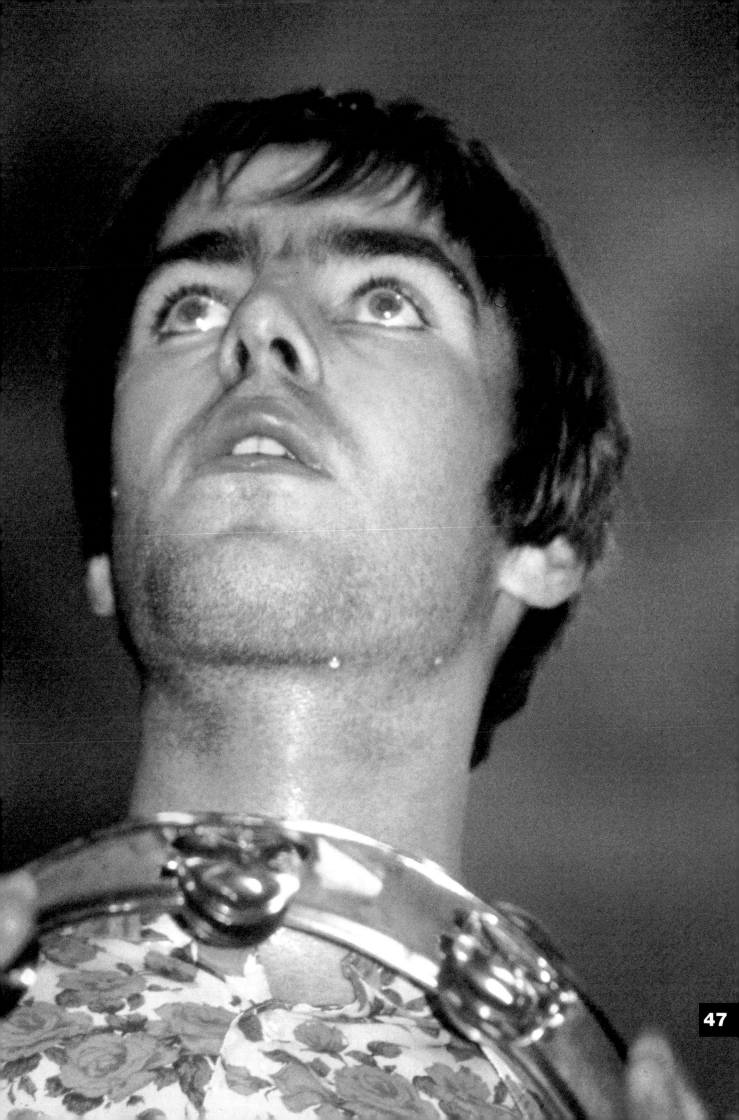

"I wouldn't sing anyone else's songs but yours and John Lennon's."

LIAM ON NOEL

"I wouldn't have anyone else sing my songs but you and John Lennon."

NOEL ON LIAM

"I tell 'em it takes years of practise to get this good. I've got a chair in my house that I practise throwing out of the window."

BONEHEAD

"Three fat blokes shouting are no competition for Oasis."

CREATION RECORDS COMMENTING ON THE THREE TENORS

"Really it's just brotherly love. I think a lot of these wild stories are made up. Privately they've got great admiration for each other. Liam looks up to Noel because he writes the songs and Noel looks up to Liam because of his voice."

PEGGY GALLAGHER

"Yeah. That's what it's all about. That's why we'll be the best band in the world, because I f***in' hate that twat there. I f***in' hate him. And I hope one day there's a release where I can smash f**k out of him, with a f***in' Rickenbacker, right on his nose!"

LIAM ON NOEL (AGAIN!)

"After I've been to Japan for two days I want to go home. Everyone's too nice - no wonder Gary Lineker went there. There's no decent food, the beer's expensive, there's no proper cigarettes, you can't get drugs, and the women are ugly."

NOEL GALLAGHER

"If we were to take John Lennon, Jimi Hendrix, Ray Davies, Steve Marriott - anybody's first two albums against my first two albums - I'm there, I'm with The Beatles."

NOEL GALLAGHER

"I'm just glad Blur aren't here...."

NOEL GALLAGHER

"I gave it to her straight, told her Damon's an idiot. Then I said "Come on, you and me, how about it? Girls who like boys and all that!""

LIAM GALLAGHER

"This is pathetic, Liam Gallagher has been banned from talking to the press as Noel is supposed to be the clever one speaking. Their capacity for saying stupid things is unbelievable."

ANDY ROSS (BLUR'S MANAGER)

"Although not being a fan of their music, I wish both Damon and Alex a long and healthy life."

NOEL GALLAGHER

"He told someone to shut up and walk home because they asked him for a number for a taxi, and that person was my mate, and I said "Don't talk to people like that who I know, just because you don't, because I'll just slap you." So we had a fight and that was it."

LIAM ON NOEL (WHAT AGAIN?)

"Manchester bored me because it's too small. You can't fart without everybody knowing about it."

NOEL GALLAGHER

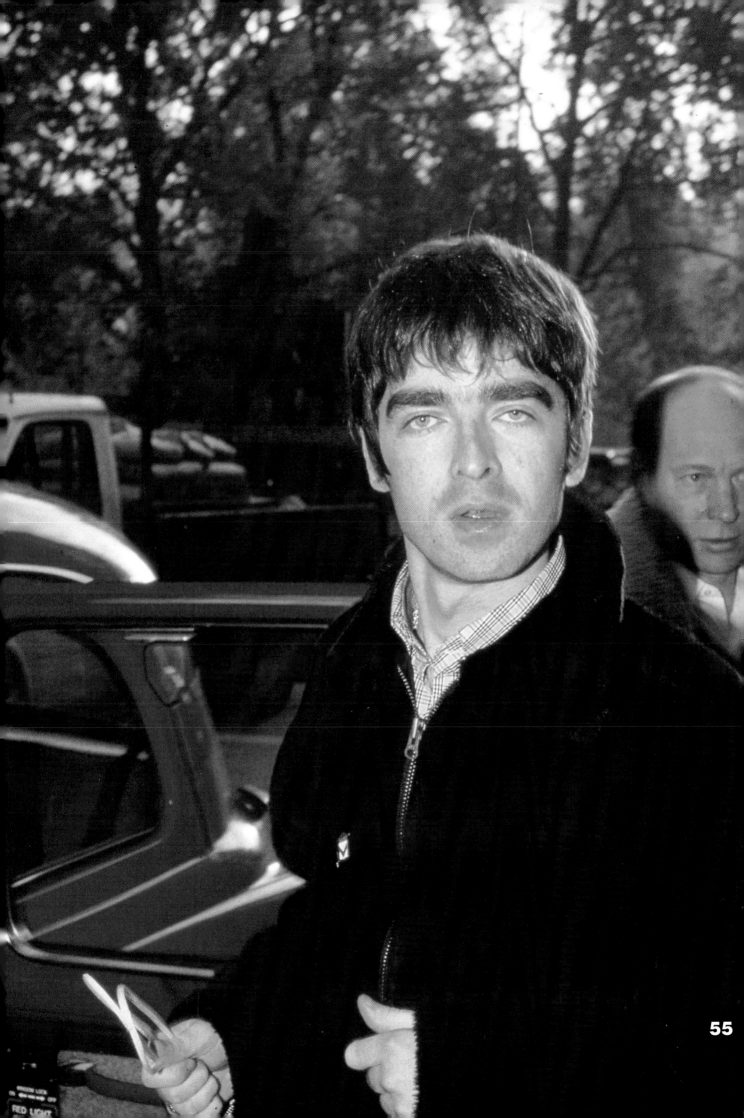

7

LOOKING AHEAD

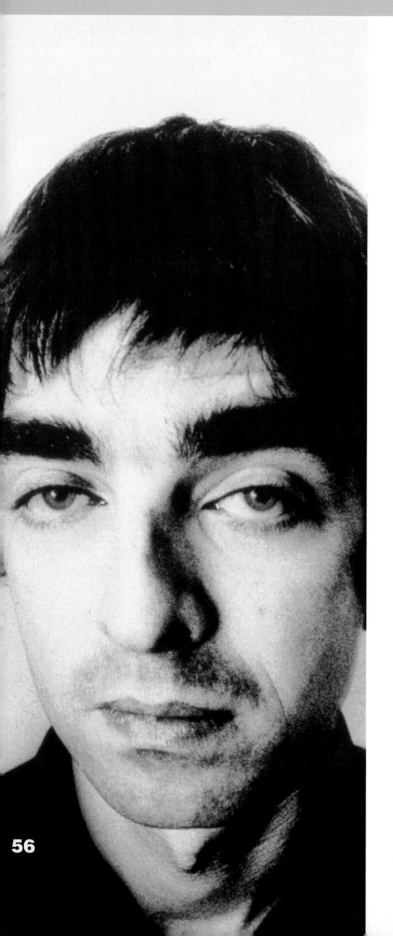

After an absolutely incredible 1995 (including a number 1 hit single, their second number 1 album and the enormous publicity generated from the "battle" with Blur), it didn't seem possible that Oasis could repeat the feat going into 1996. The New Year started very well however, with (What's The Story) Morning Glory? climbing to number 5 in the Billboard Chart and with both versions of Wonderwall enjoying both radio air play and M.T.V. rotation. In January the band played some shows in Germany and then returned to the U.K. for their first British date of the year. This was at Whitley Bay Ice Rink, Tyne & Wear.

The only bad news at this time was the announcement that sacked drummer Tony McCarroll intended to sue Oasis. Apparently Mr McCarroll believed that his expulsion from the group arose from personal differences between himself and Noel, nothing to do with his musical ability. Therefore he was claiming a case of unlawful dismissal. The whole band (including McCarroll) had signed a contract with Creation Records in 1993 that entitled everyone to an equal split of the recording royalties. This did not include publishing royalties for which Noel received 100%, being the exclusive songwriter. McCarroll's major gripe was over being excluded from the recording of the Morning Glory album.

February was a busy month for the band as tickets for their Maine Road show went on sale. 40,000 tickets

VANITY FAIR

MARCH 1997 / £2.60

LONDON
SWINGS
AGAIN

A SPECIAL 25-PAGE REPORT
HOW LONDON GOT ITS GROOVE BACK **BY DAVID KAMP**
WITH AN **EXCLUSIVE PORTFOLIO** BY LORENZO AGIUS,
DAVID LaCHAPELLE AND MICHAEL ROBERTS
OF **LIAM GALLAGHER, PATSY KENSIT, DAMIEN HIRST,**
ALEXANDER McQUEEN, JODIE KIDD, TERENCE CONRAN,
SPICE GIRLS, TONY BLAIR AND MORE.

were sold within 2 hours therefore another show was arranged "by public demand". Tickets for this second show also sold out in record time. Oasis were also busy collecting awards such as "Brats" and "Brits", entertaining the masses with their infamous speeches and comments. Pretty soon, no one was safe from a good old tongue-lashing, courtesy of Noel and "Our Kid"!

The success of Wonderwall, as a single, astonished just about everyone. The success of Wonderwall, as a cover version with the original still in the charts, defied belief. The success of the two Wonderwalls meant that the next Oasis single had to be delayed for quite a while. On February 9th, "Don't Look Back In Anger" was released. It entered the singles chart at number 1. Noel's lead vocals on the track sparked yet more rumours of brotherly hate and fuelled numerous "split" stories but as we have come to expect, it takes more than that to break up this band and Liam was going to show the world that he wasn't going anywhere just because Noel wanted to sing one song! On a monumental edition of Top Of The Pops, Oasis were permitted to play TWO songs instead of the customary one. This was a rare gesture made by the B.B.C. to only two other bands in the past, The Beatles and The Jam. As well as their number 1 hit, Oasis also played their version of Slade's "Cum On Feel The Noise".

On February 22nd, Oasis went off to the U.S.A. for their sixth (!) tour. Their numerous attempts to repeat their European success on the other side of the Atlantic had all but failed and it was starting to turn into an obsession. Critics have pointed out that Oasis had many shortcomings in front of American audiences and it was always going to be difficult to win them over. With their static live performances and undeniably British attitude, U.S. audiences were having trouble just understanding their accents (M.T.V. News put subtitles under the Gallaghers' voices during interviews!).

Oasis returned to Manchester to play the Maine Road shows at the end of April. The home of Manchester City Football Club, Maine Road's capacity of 40,000 was stretched to bursting point on both dates. Maine Road has never before been transformed into a temple of hero-worship such as this (even when the football team wins!). As the all-conquering heroes, Oasis rose to the occasion and lapped up all the admiration and more. On these two days, the band achieved an almost God-like status however, even they felt humbled playing on Maine Road's hallowed turf. It was a dream come true for the Gallaghers who had by now been recognised as the most famous Manchester City F.C. supporters in the world. Any fear of violence erupting between between rival Manchester football supporters was played down as both squads of players (Manchester City and Manchester United) were invited as special guests. Other invitations were sent to Robbie Williams, Shaun Ryder (and Black Grape), M-People, Johnny Marr, The Stone Roses and Patsy Kensit, to name a few. It was truly an event not just for Oasis, not just for Manchester City F.C., but for the whole of Manchester.

The Maine Road shows were an incredible triumph for Oasis who by now had become the biggest band in the known world, outside of the U.S.A. They didn't pass without incident including on-stage arguments and criminal activity both inside the football stadium and outside of it, however these live shows were surely the pinnacle of the band's live career to date. There were no other scheduled dates on the horizon following these shows and this was a good time for the band to take a break and to allow Noel some time off to start writing new material. They didn't stay inactive for long though. In May, Oasis announced that they were going to play two shows at Knebworth in August. It was also announced that Noel had

had been nominated for an Ivor Novello award in the Songwriter Of The Year category. Also in the same month they took part in a charity football competition which saw Oasis playing against Northern Uproar (an Oasis tribute band!) and against Blur (which they lost 2-0 although the only band members playing in this match were Liam and Guigsy).

More controversy was soon to follow on numerous fronts. Firstly it was announced that Oasis would be playing the August festival at Loch Lomond. This got the month of June off to a great start (!) as local residents protested en masse. The main cause for their concern was the prospect of 80,000 fans descending on the village of Balloch. They were particularly bothered by the fact that Balloch is alleged to have just one public toilet. Festival promoters assured the presence of on-site lavatories in abundance and the protests died down. The second controversial incident was when Noel was informed that he had won the Ivor Novello award for which he had been nominated. The problem was that Blur had won the same award! Noel was furious and failed to show at the ceremony, claiming that it was a cheap publicity stunt and that he would not share an award with "them twats"! In the event, Blur didn't show either and for the first time an Ivor Novello award went unclaimed.

There have been numerous other controversies since then including more Noel/Liam "bust ups", Liam's stormy relationship with Patsy Kensit and the Oasis "split" which occurred a few months later on tour in the U.S. It seems you just can't keep a good band down....

8

Oasis have become almost as famous for their behaviour and comments off stage as they have for their music and performances on it. The relationship between Oasis and the music press has always been stormy to say the least. However, after the success of the second album, Oasis (and in particular the Gallaghers and their respective female companions) stopped being a concern for just the music press as they entered the realm of "public domain". These days you will be more likely to read about their exploits and most recent controversial comments in the tabloid press.

Such is the popularity and enormity of their achievements (particularly in the U.K.) that they are front page news, whatever they seem to get up to. Liam Gallagher is a particular favourite with the world's news mongers who still view him as little more than a football hooligan who happens to have a talented brother, Noel is regarded as more of a musical personality who not only has had to carry his brother but very often is held responsible for his actions. Whatever your opinion of Noel and Liam's relationship with each other and with the press, I think most people would agree that the world would be a rather boring place without them!

Now you can make up your own mind. The following interview took place between Noel, Liam and a European

63

Rock Journalist just following the release of (What's The Story) Morning Glory? in October 1995.

Do you still think of yourselves as a Manchester band....

NOEL "What's a Manchester band?"

LIAM "It's a band that comes from Manchester, right?"

You know: Inspiral Carpets, Happy Mondays, Oasis....Manchester bands, right?

NOEL "Well we come from Manchester, no one can change that. But there's more to life than just Manchester. And there's more to Oasis than just Manchester."

What do you think of the current Manchester scene....

NOEL "I don't think there is a current Manchester "scene". It's a myth of our time. Manchester has seen it's fair share of good bands, of which I hope we're one, but there's been loads of other decent bands from places outside of Manchester, so it really doesn't bother me and to be quite honest I get pissed off having to talk about Manchester all the time. It's the people that make the bands; you know the musicians, the labels, the fans. Not the city which is just roads and concrete...."

LIAM "And a couple of football grounds."

Some people are saying that you've made your name on the back of the Manchester scene, and now you're turning your backs on it....

LIAM "That's crap, right? We've just moved on, right? Them people don't know f**k all about it. They go on about Manchester this and Manchester that and they've never even been there right? We've lived it for long enough, and I can tell you that it's shite! I don't owe anyone in Manchester anything; I love City and I've got friends there but as for feeling guilty or anything...."

NOEL "He's never felt guilty about anything before so I don't suppose this is any different."

Okay, lets talk about the new album....

LIAM "Thank f**k for that!"

How do you think it differs from Definitely Maybe....

NOEL "Well it's still only our second album so there's gonna be some similarities. We've got a different drummer on this one, but it's basically the same band.

The main differences are in what we're trying to achieve this time, instead of just doing Definitely Maybe Part 2. That would have been really boring and predictable so I thought f**k it, this one's gonna be different and I think it is."

I've heard some people say it's heavier....

LIAM "What the f**k does that mean? We ain't a heavy band, we ain't Metal or anything. This album ain't a heavy album in that way is it?"

I suppose it's more of a rock album than the last one....

NOEL "You could be right. But I think there's enough of all sorts on this one to please most people especially ourselves, which is the main thing."

LIAM "This album's definitely up for it! It's gonna blow a few people right out of the water I can promise you...."

People like Blur....

NOEL "Who?"

LIAM "I never knew them twats were still going. I've not heard f**k all about them lately and as far as I'm concerned it's good riddance! I knew they wouldn't last anyway."

I don't think they're finished just yet....

LIAM "This album will finish them. They can't live with us and everyone knows it."

NOEL "Look, the Blur thing is over right? We don't care what they do anymore. They started it in the first place and now we've finished it everyone thinks we give a shit about them. Well we don't!"

LIAM "Look it's not about Blur, right? It's about us, right? The Blur thing is f***in' dead now, just like Blur. We don't need to kill them anymore, they managed to kill themselves without any help from us."

What about the Gallagher brothers, has your relationship changed at all....

LIAM "No man, we're sweet. Me and him are sweet but people keep saying shite about us and they don't know the story. It's f***in' pathetic man. I haven't hit him for ages man, no lie. We've not had any reason to argue for ages man, it's scary!"

NOEL "We work so f***in' hard we never get a chance to do half the shit we read about. It's funny, it's f***in' sad too. Papers and shit have not got a clue about us and still they write the same stories, every day of every f***in' week. Me and our kid, we just laugh."

LIAM "All the way to the bank man, all the way to the bank."

Noel, what about the new album? Much has been said about the fact that you sing on a song and that Liam is not happy about it....

LIAM "That's bollocks."

NOEL "We're bigger than that. He's bigger than that, and I'm bigger than that. People have said I only wrote the song to piss him off but that's ridiculous. I don't need to write a song to piss our kid off! I can piss him off any time I want, no problem. So every time I read that it just makes me laugh."

LIAM "It never pissed me off anyway, it's cool cos when we do it live I can f**k off stage and have a beer man! Now that's pretty cool, eh?"

So you're not breaking up over it? I heard a rumour....

LIAM "F**k your rumours man! We ain't splitting up, I ain't pissed off and that's the end of it. Right?"

NOEL "We've been splitting up since day one, if you believe everything you read. It's more bull shit and I'm not losing any sleep over it."

What about Guigsy? Is he still in Oasis....

NOEL "Guigsy needs a rest. There is no Oasis without him so to answer your question, YES!"

But he's not going with you to the States is he.....

NOEL "No he's not, but he'll be back. He's having a few months off and then he'll be back. He's sweet about it and it won't be a problem. He's under doctor's orders and all that so we'll have to go without him but it won't change anything. He's still our bass player, simple as that."

It appears to be an obsession, your attempt to make it in the States....

NOEL "Is that what it looks like to you?"

Yes....

NOEL "Well that's an honest opinion and I respect that, but it's not the case. We're trying to make this band the biggest on the planet, and it can't be done unless you go to America. It's not the be all and end all, but it is a part of it just like Australia is or Britain is or Japan is. It's just another country, that's all. We may never get what we want over there, but we're gonna try for it. And if it's just not meant to be, then so be it."

LIAM "We f***in' love it man. Those Yanks are up for it I tell ya, they're mad for it! We'll keep going over there until they get the message, and if they don't well at least we're having a good time trying!"

NOEL "That's one of the problems in Britain. People don't see further than their back garden. There's a whole world out there that's got nothing to do with Britain, or even Manchester or any Manchester "scene". Some people are just happy to be in a little band, you know indie or rock or whatever, and just play all the same gigs and never go anywhere. Well we're not like that. We're bigger than all that and we're gonna be bigger in a lot more places by the time it's all over. Yeah, we could just be big in Britain or Europe and settle for that. But until you move away and see the States and Japan and places like that, you'll never realise your full potential. And that's what drove me to join this band in the first place. We've got a lot of potential that is yet to be fulfilled."

69

9

Oasis moved into 1997 with high hopes for the coming year. The previous two years had turned out far better than anyone (including Creation Records, the music press, the fans and even the band themselves) could possibly have imagined. There had been more than a few lows along the way: the cancellation of the U.S. tour due to Liam's alleged "house hunting", constant rumours of a split, arrests for various drug-related offences, more fights between Noel and Liam, a perpetual running battle with the tabloid press and various other problems that had dogged the band. Even Bonehead had got in on the act with a story that involved an alleged threat to shoot someone! Oasis were well and truly a part of every day life and had been for some time.

Oasis are without doubt the ultimate "indie" band. Emerging from the legendary Manchester scene in the wake of The Happy Mondays, The Stone Roses and most significantly of all, the Inspiral Carpets, their success has long since transcended and completely overtaken any of their so-called rivals. The international achievements of this band, both commercially and critically, have totally rewritten the rule books. Oasis have proved that there are no limits on what can be accomplished and have subsequently left the ranks of the indie masses. They are now "international rock superstars" and look set to remain that way for a long time to come.

As 1997 has now started to unfold,

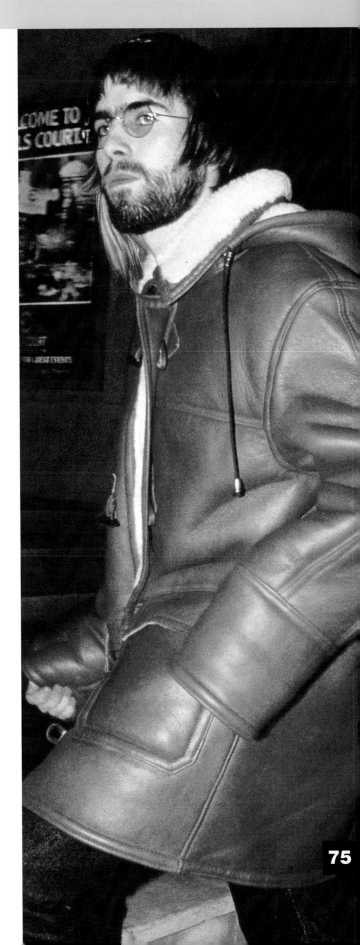

one can only see more success on the horizon for Britain's biggest band. The year started quietly (if that could be possible!) with many people wondering if the Oasis machine had finally ground to halt. NO CHANCE! Both Gallaghers married their respective "other halves" in somewhat controversial fashion; the on/off nature of Liam and Patsy's wedding in particular had the entire nation waiting with bated breath and when it finally did happen, neither Noel nor Peggy Gallagher were present at the ceremony. Nevertheless, it spawned a thousand (give or take nine hundred or so) newspaper headlines, and their marital status is still a source of endless media fascination.

The release of the third official Oasis album will surely be one of the music industry's highlights of 1997. It seems like a lifetime ago that they started recording it at the world famous Abbey Road studios. I can't think of a more eagerly-awaited and long overdue product in the entire history of recorded music. Can it possibly emulate the success of it's two predecessors? Many people feel that it will be the true test for Oasis. That we will find out once and for all if they really can fulfil the potential that they seem to possess in abundance. I suppose that only time will tell. Well, not quite. We have had a small indication of what's to come with the release of the single "D'you Know What I Mean?", the first new Oasis release of any kind for over 12 months. It still hasn't quite had time to grow on me, but initial listening makes me think of....err....Oasis. Yes, this seems to be a song that can sit right alongside "Champagne Supernova" or "Some Might Say" as an anthemic rocker in true Gallagher style. It MUST be a big hit and surely the new album will be no different. The video is equally spectacular, full of military helicopters and obviously costing a fortune to make. Someone commented to me that it was like "Full Metal Jacket" gone MAD FOR IT! Oasis have done it again.

Speaking of the new album, did you see the fuss in the newspapers when they took the pictures for the front cover? The Sun (Britain's largest tabloid) went berserk, trying to decipher and analyse the imagery. They really should have known better, but I suppose it proved to be yet more much-needed (?) publicity, catapulting the group back on to the front pages of just about every national newspaper. With it's surreal composition, the picture obviously contained many references to The Beatles and The Who. So where's the surprise?

Ah yes, the tired old Beatles tag. Look, Oasis are NOT the new Beatles. I think everyone knows that by now. No one could ever repeat the timeless success or importance of The Beatles, the greatest Rock and Roll band of all time. But there never has been a musical group of any sort that has not been influenced by The Beatles, and Oasis are no different. They just seem to be more influenced by them than most. What's wrong with that? At the end of the day, the music of Oasis will stand or fall on it's own merits or shortcomings and I'm sure Noel wouldn't want it any other way.

But there's so much more to the Oasis legend than just music. Take, for example, the most recent controversy surrounding an interview with both Noel and Liam (published in a rather popular U.K. music paper). The brothers Gallagher comment on just about everything including life, the universe and our creator (that's God to you!). Noel sparked off yet more fury with a quote that Oasis are more important than religion, "When was the last time God played Knebworth?" he inquired. Soon after, a church spokesman replied "Mr Gallagher, God doesn't play Knebworth, He created it!" Religion 1 Oasis 0, but we've not even reached half-time and I'm sure Noel can conjure up an equaliser from somewhere. Liam stated that yes, he did believe in extraterrestrial life but that he was smarter than any "goggle-eyed alien" and that even though they may well possess far superior technology and a greater understanding of the universe, he'd "probably do their heads in" because "they haven't got a f***in' clue"! The thought of an intergalactic explorer travelling millions of light years across the vast expanses of the cosmos to arrive at planet Earth and then uttering the immortal line (through a sub-space universal translator of course) "Take me to your Liam" just doesn't quite wash with me. The phrase "Liam Gallagher, Spokesman of a Generation" is questionable at best. "Liam Gallagher, Spokesman of the Human Race"....err....I don't think so.

So that's it. The Oasis Chronicles are complete. Well, sort of. For now we can do no more than just reflect on the last few years, waiting all the while for the next album to emerge. One thing is for sure, Noel and Liam's love/hate relationship will not split the band as easily as many had predicted. Oasis have proved that they are more than just one or two album wonders and that their story is not over yet. Times have changed and time has dragged Oasis along to the next level, they've even put their bitter rivalry with Blur to one side (Oasis and Blur appeared on the same bill, supporting U2 in the U.S.A.)! Which brings me back to the question, "Will Oasis ever conquer the States?" The editor of the world's biggest pop music magazine recently told me that "....it's only a matter of time. They're too much like The Beatles to not make it over there. It's inevitable." I happen to agree with him. It seems with every passing episode in the amazing history of Oasis, they're getting closer and closer to their goal. America will be brought to heel one way or another, but for now it's time I shut up and let their music do the talking....Definitely....err....maybe....err....

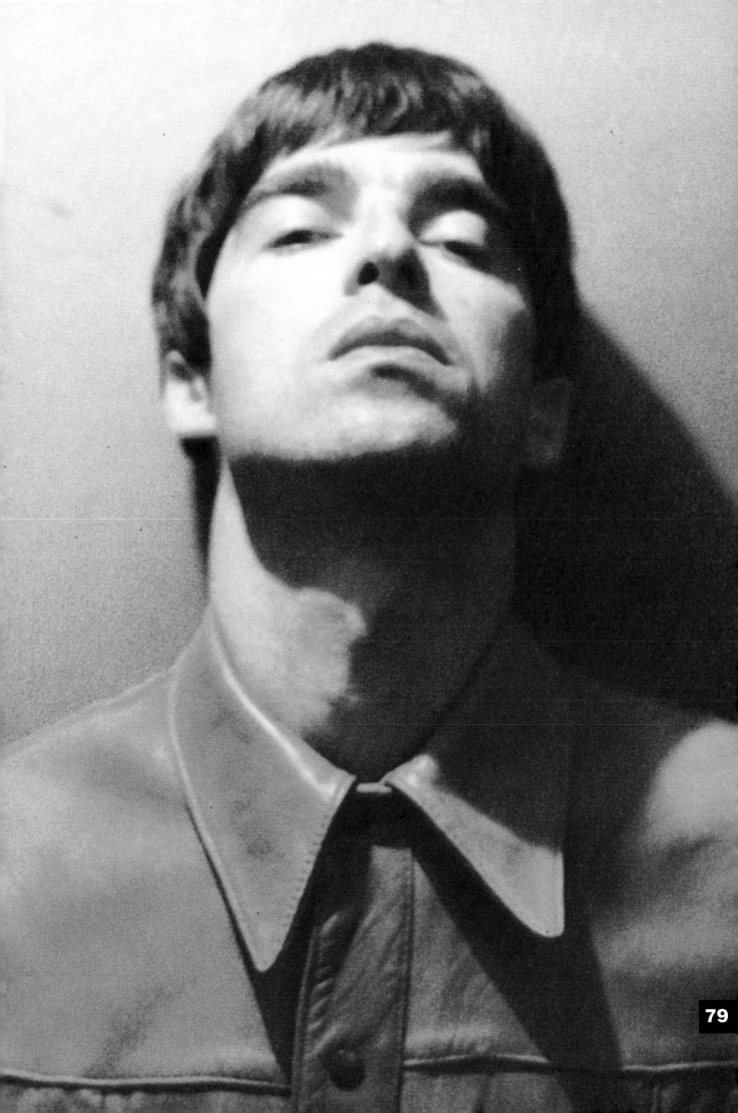

ACKNOWLEDGMENTS

Company executive - Richard Driscoll.
Arrowhead executive - David Richter.
Designed by Daniel Wilkins.
Edited, copywritten + story by David Richter + Ski Newton.

All photographs in this work are courtesy of Visual Entertainment Archives Inc. New York U.S.A.